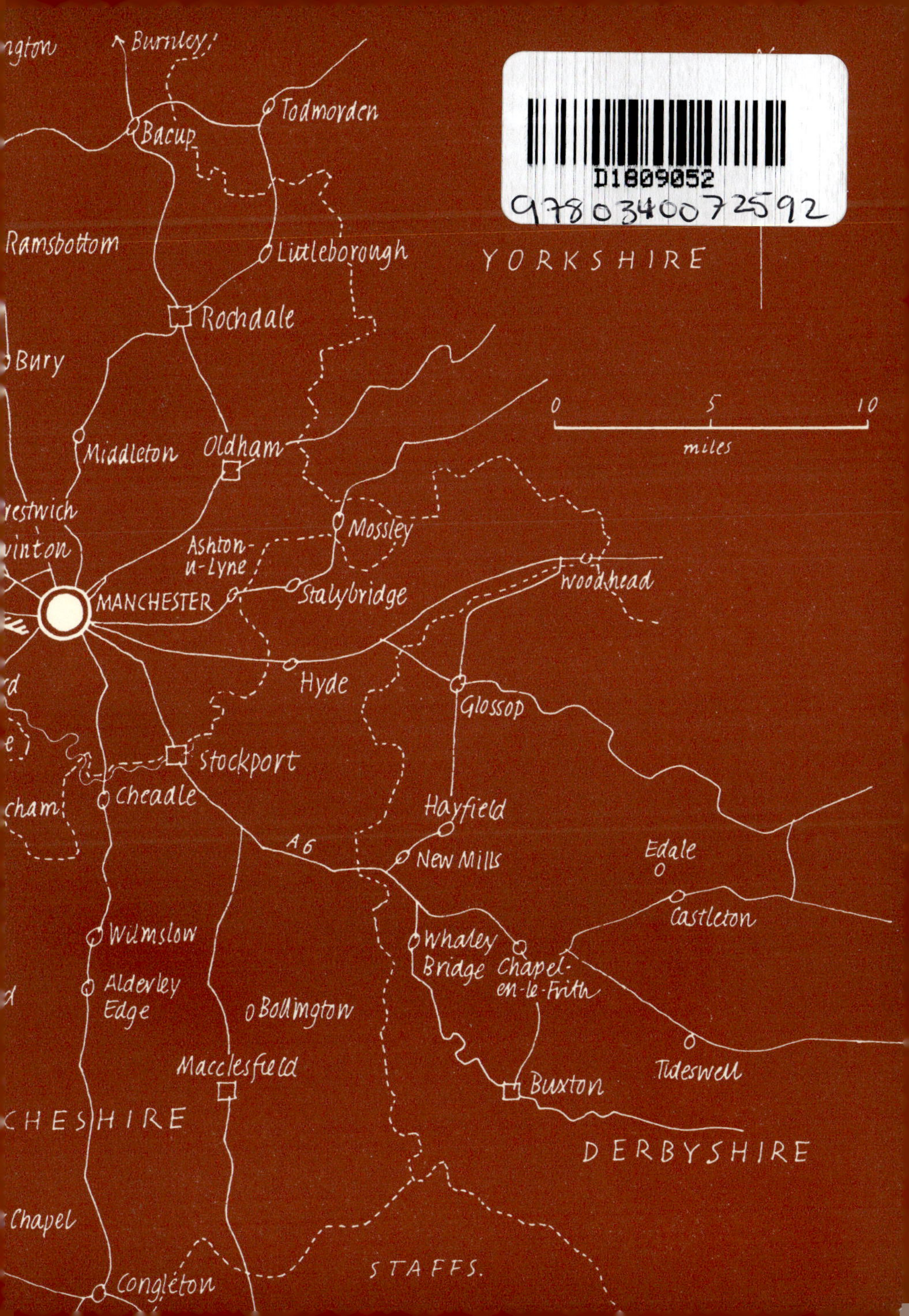

ngton
Burnley
Bacup
Todmorden
Ramsbottom
Littleborough
YORKSHIRE
Rochdale
Bury
0   5   10
miles
Middleton
Oldham
restwich
vinton
Mossley
Ashton-
u-Lyne
MANCHESTER
Stalybridge
Woodhead
Hyde
Glossop
d
e.)
Stockport
cham
Cheadle
Hayfield
Edale
A 6
New Mills
Castleton
Wilmslow
Whaley
Bridge
Chapel-
en-le-Frith
Alderley
Edge
Bollington
Macclesfield
Tideswell
Buxton
CHESHIRE
DERBYSHIRE
Chapel
STAFFS.
Congleton

*It happened*
*round Manchester*

TOPICS IN REGIONAL HISTORY

Advisory editors
W. H. Shercliff
N. J. Frangopulo

*Cover: Pablo Fanque's circus
at Rochdale, 1843*

*Belle Vue Zoo Park, Manchester, from the air*

IT HAPPENED ROUND MANCHESTER

# Entertainments

W. H. Shercliff

University of
London Press Ltd

SBN 340 07259 8



University of London Press Ltd
St Paul's House, Warwick Lane, London EC4
Designed by Gerald Wilkinson
Printed and bound in Great Britain by
C. Tinling & Co. Ltd, Liverpool, London and Prescot

# Contents

# Acknowledgments

The author is indebted to the following for permission to quote
from copyright publications: J. M. Dent and Sons Ltd for material
from J. F. Russell and J. H. Elliot, *The Brass Band Movement*
(page 32); MacGibbon and Kee Ltd for material from C. B. Rees,
*One Hundred Years of the Hallé* (page 38); Campbell Connelly
and Co. Ltd for two verses of the song 'In my little bottom drawer'
(page 41).
Cordial thanks are also due to the following for the use of
illustrations: Aerofilms Ltd (frontispiece); Granada Television
(page 9); the Local History Library, Manchester Public Libraries
(pages 13, 14, 15, 17 above, 19, 21, 23, 37 left, 39, 43, 44, 46,
48, 49, 51, 53 below); *Rochdale Observer* (page 17 below); the
Raymond Mander and Joe Mitchenson Theatre Collection (page
24); the City Engineer, Manchester Corporation (page 27); *The
Guardian* (page 29); Belle Vue (Manchester) Ltd (page 33: photo
Park Pictures); *Rossendale Free Press* (page 35); Manchester City
Art Galleries and Museums (page 36); Hallé Concerts Society
(pages 37 right: photo Klaus Hennch, Zurich, and 38: photo
S G Photography); Mr Clifford C. Ashton (cover, from an original
bill in Rochdale Public Library, and page 40); Associated
Electrical Industries Ltd (page 53 above); the BBC (page 61).

# Introduction

This series of books will help you to find out more about the history of the region round Manchester. This region has a special unity of its own. A man who lives in Wilmslow may work in Trafford Park, go to Hallé concerts in Manchester and support Stockport Football Club. His life is very much bound up with the activities of the whole region, as well as with those of his immediate home district. Journeys to work, to go shopping, to seek entertainment, to improve his education, may take him to many different parts of the region, which contains a living society. In this series we introduce a number of topics important to our life here, and show how we have reached our present stage of development.

Leisure time pursuits are just as much a part of the history of a region as how people have earned their living and met their daily needs. This book is about those spectacles which the showmen of the past, as well as the present, have presented to all kinds of people in this region. Games and sports, festivals and fairs, local customs and entertainments in private houses, may be described in future books in the series.

It is not possible to give in detail the history of every theatre, cinema or musical society in the region. Examples have been taken to illustrate the general interest of the subject and show how you can find out more about your own local entertainments. Some, such as television and broadcasting or zoological gardens, have to be organised on a regional basis, and for these Manchester is the natural centre. Others, such as brass bands or amateur theatres, are purely local in character. Choral societies and repertory theatres require more support than small towns can give and therefore tend to flourish in larger towns.

For a full understanding of the subject, many kinds of entertainment must be explored. We hope that this book will launch you on such a voyage of exploration.

W.H.S.

N.J.F.

NOTE – The books and pamphlets listed on page 62 are numbered and arranged in the order of the chapters and subjects in this book. Your local library should be able to obtain them for you. Other books and sources are mentioned in the text of this book.

# 1 Television versus cosmorama

The Lancashire and Cheshire man has often put the same zest into his pleasures and amusements as he has into his daily work. The towns of the North are renowned for their support for sport, for classical and popular music, for drama and other forms of organised entertainment. Isobel Baillie, Kathleen Ferrier, John Ogdon are as renowned in the world of music as Bobby Charlton, Brian Statham or Joe Brown, champions of football, cricket and mountain climbing, in that of sport.

Today, boys and girls may have a choice of three different television programmes. They can have the terror of an earthquake, the beauty of a bay or mountain, or the latest personality in the news brought right into their sitting-room within a few hours of the event. While the viewer does not have to stir from his fireside, for the producer the job of presenting his material is a complicated one. He has to make use of the age-old skills of actor, dancer, singer and musician as well as the technical masterpieces of our present age, such as the film camera, the videotape recorder and the television camera. In earlier ages a boy or girl would have to go to a town to be entertained, and great spectacles were much harder to present. Events and scenes could not be so reliably, quickly or clearly reported. It is a far cry from some of the spectacles available in 1850 to a modern TV magazine programme.

As you know, Granada's twenty- to thirty-minute daily magazine programme 'Scene' reports on matters of interest both inside and outside our region. It may contain live interviews with people in the news, sometimes pre-recorded in a London studio where the cameras are remotely controlled from Manchester. Pieces of film taken by outside units, interviews, news items and other comments are linked by two announcers alternating. The items are decided on during the day. Scripts are prepared after the necessary work has been done to find the facts and pictures needed. Pictures and voices have to be mixed in harmony with one another. A rehearsal takes place which is very important for timing the items, linking them to one another and judging their success.

In the sound-proof control room during rehearsal six people act under the instructions of the director. Cameramen and announcers in the studio below, visible through a great window, obey his instructions also. A red ring flashes round one of the seven monitors showing the picture which is being used. The picture may come live from the studio, or from the teleciné room where films are put on at exactly the right moment, or from another room where still pictures and captions (that is titles, headings, cartoons or drawings) already prepared during the day are photographed as needed. In a room behind the control room a sound-technician operates tape recorders and gramophones. Here musical background and sound effects are provided.

With the aid of this array of monitors, and what he can see in the studio below, the key man, the director, selects what he wants during rehearsal like the conductor of an orchestra. He tells the announcers to alter their expression, or decides when to cut out from a piece of film. A girl armed with stop watches helps him with the timing. The teamwork which goes into making such an entertainment is most impressive and there is much friendly chaffing between the research workers, technicians and producer. Curt instructions and comments come over the intercom microphone: 'Teleciné's having trouble', 'Wonderful artiste, she uses her whole body', 'That's no use for a fade out'. Suddenly the live show is finished, the lights go off and the work of this particular team is ended for the day. But tomorrow they will be searching for another nine or ten interesting items for the programme.

Now look back in contrast to an earlier period, 1850, when your great-great-grandfathers were alive and when already there was a large population in the Manchester area. Much entertainment was found in the public houses and in gin palaces and streets. Long working hours, even for children, limited leisure; and Saturday afternoon was only just becoming a holiday for some.

As advertisements show, a father could take his boy and girl to the Free Trade Hall (then a wooden building) to a show that the promoters called *cosmorama*. Behind this was the same idea as underlies television. Cosmorama means views of the world and television means views of distant objects. But instead of using the magic eye of a camera the staff and students of the Manchester School of Design had painted enormous coloured pictures of beautiful scenes – some over ten feet by fourteen feet. Two elaborate dioramas were included. A diorama was an early attempt to bring pictures to life by clever use of direct and reflected light. Real objects as well as pictorial backgrounds were displayed in curtained cubicles to give a three-dimensional effect. One represented the mountains, river valley and rocks of the Sacramento Valley of California by moonlight (the mysterious Golden West of the USA). The other, more elaborate, was of the interior of St Peter's, Rome, which could be shown in a series of scenes representing different times of the day by means of different lighting and various painted drops. It was given a place of honour on the stage in the show, and was approached down a piazza (or public square) with other scenes in alcoves down either side. Statues and an elaborate fountain with twelve jets playing completed the effect. The organ already in the building was concealed behind the stage. The *Manchester Guardian* describes the spectacle in the rather flowery language of the period.

'There at stated times the drop scene of the platform rises to the solemn strains of the organ . . . revealing to the spectator the interior of that first of Catholic temples. . . . It is first seen by the light of the full moon pouring its mild radiance through the windows of the clerestory. The effect is fine. The moon goes down; the rising sun brings column and arch, architrave and capital into clearer view and higher light. . . . But another dioramic change passes over the scene. Day closes and suddenly the whole of the spacious interior is illuminated by an immense cross of brilliant lamps suspended under the central dome. The before silent and empty space is now at once peopled by a vast throng of the devout kneeling and uncovered . . . the pealing organ pours forth . . . the effect is for the moment quite electric.'

# POMONA GARDENS
## CORNBROOK, HULME.

### GRAND GALA NIGHTS
### EVERY MONDAY EVENING, DURING THE SUMMER SEASON.

#### SPLENDID REPRESENTATION OF THE

# ERUPTION OF MOUNT VESUVIUS,

As it occurred in 1849, the most terrific on record. The View is taken from the Magnificent Bay of Naples; the Water giving distance and beauty to the Picture, and forms a happy junction of Nature and Art. This Splendid Picture has been painted and erected under the Superintendence of the Celebrated Artist, Mr. A. F. Tait, and extends the whole Length of the Lake, covering upwards of 20,000 square yards of Canvass, and is one of
### The Largest ever Erected in England.
The MANCHESTER BRASS BAND will be in attendance and p'ay some of the most Fashionable Airs, Overtures, &c. The Gardens will be Brilliantly Illuminated with Variegated Lamps, &c.
### ADMISSION, 1s. CHILDREN, HALF-PRICE.
The Proprietor of the above Gardens begs respectfully to announce that they are OPEN DAILY for the reception of Visitors, and will be found admirably calculated to afford enjoyment to every class of the community. Families, Ladies and Strangers visiting Manchester will be highly delighted with a Visit to these Gardens. The Magic Bridge, Gymnasium, Flying Swings, Bowling Green, Rifle Shooting Gallery, Boats on the IRWELL, Beautiful Flower Beds, Statues, Romantic Walks, Extensive Pasture Grounds, and Promenade will afford to
...nd Inrenilec

*An announcement for an exciting spectacle, 1850*

Perhaps the children of 1850 might have agreed with the reporter who went on to say that this show lacked living and human interest. The showman in fact later brought in the Italian opera singers who were performing at the neighbouring new Theatre Royal. They sang appropriate solos, duets and trios in between the hours of opening of the diorama. Panoramas continued till the 1890s when Niagara was shown, and the battle of Trafalgar, but the invention of the moving film made so many square yards of painting unnecessary.

Two other exciting spectacles could be seen which any boy or girl would enjoy. At Buile Hill, Pendleton (still the home of scientific wonders as it is now a science museum), on the roof of the home of John Potter, Edward Staites in the evenings demonstrated the wonders of the new electric light. Weather permitting he could focus his great beam on the clock of the Old Church (now Manchester Cathedral) or Lancashire Independent College (Northern Congregational College) four miles away in the fields of Withington. At Pomona Gardens, Hulme, as the bill shows, the wonders of the bay of Naples, with an eruption of Vesuvius represented by a fine burst of fireworks, could be seen. This was first on display during the Whitweek holidays and later throughout the summer with early shows for 'juveniles'.

Thus were ingenuity and energy brought to bear on popular entertainments, aided by whatever science and art could at that time provide.

*South-west view of Pomona Gardens, 1875*

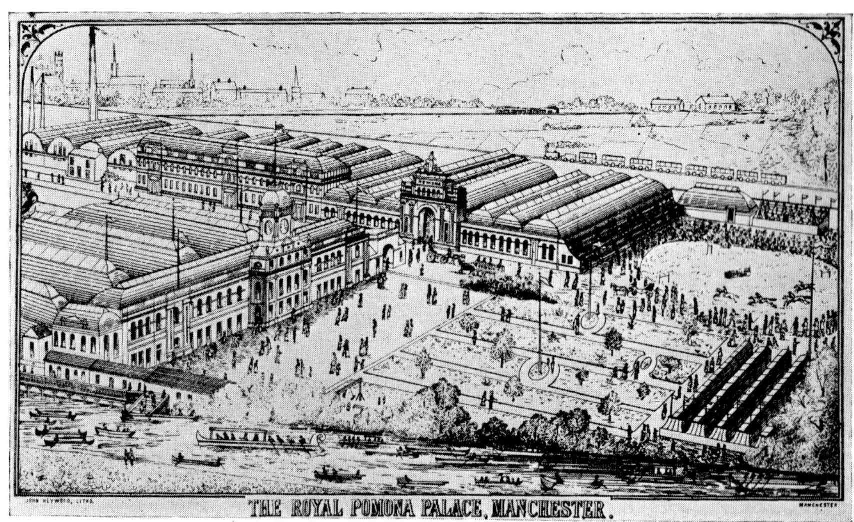

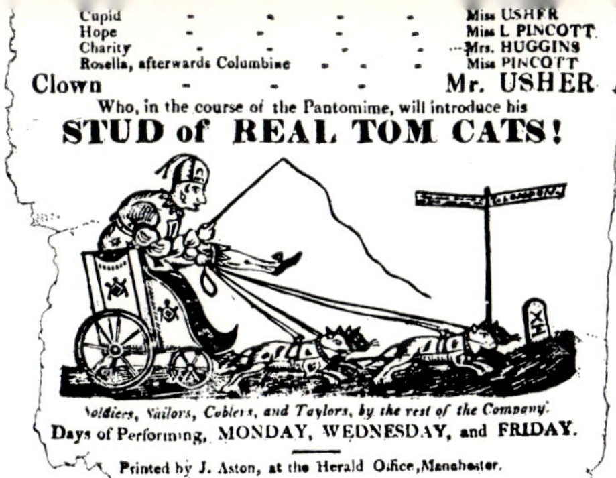


# 2 Dramatic entertainments

Men have put on costume and acted to entertain from the earliest times. The voice raised in anger, the infectious chuckle have drawn an audience round them whether players were performing on the wagon on which medieval miracle plays were acted, or the sophisticated stage of a modern theatre.

## MUMMERS' PLAYS

There is no trace now of mystery or miracle plays being acted nearer than Chester, but one form of the old popular drama survives in the mummers' plays. Some of the characters from these plays which dealt with the legends of St George or of Robin Hood appeared in the performances at festivals at Christmas or Easter or on Lady Day (25 March).

Many versions of the play of which St George is the central character were handed down in different towns and villages. Basically the play represents the rite of spring, or death and resurrection. Besides St George other characters were either a dragon or prince or a character called the Slasher, and sometimes Hector, the champion of the prince. There was usually a doctor who raised the dead to life, the devil, and, in Cheshire, Old Hob, a horse's head from a knacker's yard, the bones strung together so that the mouth worked and the teeth could make a horrific bite. The head was decorated and carried on a pole. The fool with his byplay and buffeting of spectators with a pig's bladder on a stick helped the action along. A version of the play is given in Harland's *Lancashire Legends*. Here is an extract to give the flavour of the doggerel verse.

*Enter Slasher to St George.*

SLASHER    I am a valiant soldier, and Slasher is my name;
With sword and buckler by my side, I hope to win the game;
And for to fight with me I see thou art not able,
So with my trusty broad-sword I soon will thee disable.

ST GEORGE  Disable! disable! it lies not in thy power,
For with my glittering sword and spear I soon will thee devour,
Stand off, Slasher! Let no more be said,
For if I draw my sword I'm sure to break thy head.

Sim Schofield in his book *Short stories about Failsworth folk* recalls learning the various parts in the play in his youth, and practising with his tin sword and horn.

We used to practise the piece in Bill Middleton's big loomhouse. 'Old Bill' took kindly to us lads, and he used to coach us whilst weaving at his loom, saying, 'Theaw spakes thy words badly, lad: theaw mun get some swine's grace (grease) and grace thy lips.'

This play is still performed by the boys of Rochdale Grammar School, as the picture shows.

The best version of the play is that compiled for the School by John Priestnall and William E. Mitchell of Rochdale, entitled *The play of St George, the Knights and the Dragon* (1), which contains all the features of the various early versions and includes stage directions. E. K. Chambers in *The Medieval Stage* refers to twenty-nine printed versions. A very interesting one, printed in the form of a chap-book, entitled *The Peace Egg*, by T. Pearson, printer of Chadderton Street, Manchester, is to be found in the Manchester Reference Library. This has pictures of the chief characters, helpful if you want to adopt the traditional costume.

Does your school or district ever perform this rousing play?

*Right : Title page of* The Peace Egg, *a little pamphlet printed in the early nineteenth century*
*Below : Rochdale Grammar School boys in the parts of St George, the Dragon and the Devil, 1967*

THE
PEACE EGG.
Printed and Published by
T. PEARSON, Printer, Chadderton-st., Oldham Road.

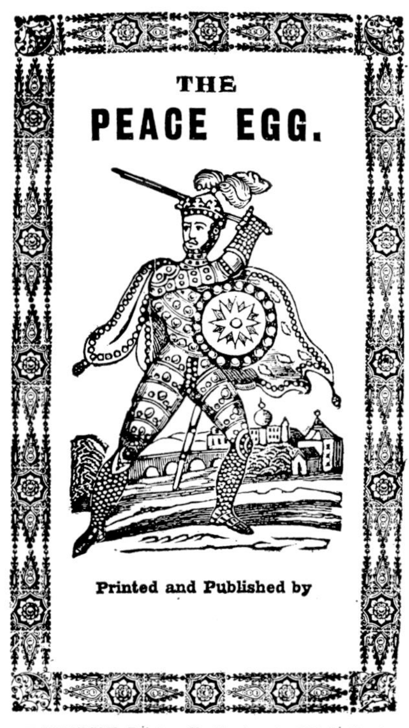

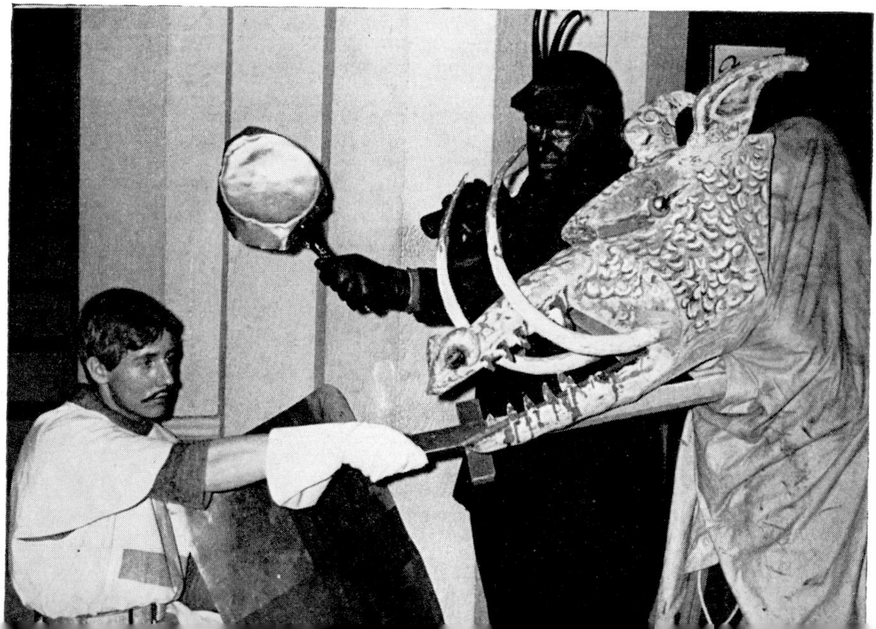

## THE FIRST THEATRES

Organised entertainment on the public stage is first known in Manchester in the eighteenth century. The first local playbill which has been preserved shows a play called *The Recruiting Officer* being performed at the Exchange in the Market Square about 1743. Soon after this in 1750 the first theatre was erected at Marsden Street, a modest square building, which was also used for cockfighting. Plays were put on in Salford at the Riding School and in Hill-gate, Stockport, in the 1760s. A stock company run by Mr Whitley, a great touring theatrical manager, worked in Manchester at this time, performing the old stock tragedies, comedies, even pantomimes, and several of Shakespeare's plays. By 1775 a licensed playhouse in Manchester was being discussed, and by 1800 small theatres were established in Lancashire towns such as Rochdale and Wigan.

Some feared the working classes would be distracted from their work and their morals be corrupted by plays such as *The Beggar's Opera*. Others whose views won the day thought 'cheerful rational amusements' would drive out the melancholy faith of Methodism. Thus the first Theatre Royal in Manchester was built at the junction of York Street and Spring Gardens. It cost three shillings for places in the boxes, two shillings in the pit and one shilling in the gallery. Lighting was by means of oil and candles, so there could be no spotlights. Great actors and actresses such as J. P. Kemble and Mrs Siddons appeared in Manchester, which was in close touch with London and other provincial theatres. Musical pieces, ballad operas and farces were included. During the wars with France patriotic songs were put in the bill and stirring plays such as Shakespeare's *Henry V* were performed. Pantomimes included a new version of *The Lancashire Witches* with local scenes and music by the organist of St Ann's Church. Grimaldi, already a skilled dancer, singer and acrobat,

*The Theatre Royal in Peter Street, Manchester, about 1850*

became probably the greatest English clown. In his famous pantomime *Mother Goose* he emphasised the story and made the part of the clown much more important. This pantomime appeared in Manchester in 1808. Tumbling, acrobatics and tight-rope walking were also featured. Animals were often brought on the stage, and in 1819 (as the poster on page 15 shows) Mr Usher, a famous clown, claimed to drive a troupe of tom cats – surely a difficult feat.

## THE THEATRE IN MANCHESTER

It is not possible to give here a detailed history of all the theatres in Manchester, but suggestions for further reading on the subject will be found on page 62 (2, 3 and 4). Fortunately, from the eighteenth century very full collections of playbills and programmes have been preserved in libraries. Reviews of first performances of plays can be found in local newspapers once the dates of performance are known.

If you read these you can find out what the critics thought on the first night, which is not necessarily the same as what the public thought. It would be a fascinating piece of research to take one of the theatres in the region, study the performances held there and so follow its life story. Theatres were opened in most of the towns of the region in the eighteenth and early nineteenth centuries. What can you find out about your nearest theatre? The building may still be there, even if the theatre has closed.

In Manchester the Theatre Royal moved to its third and present building in 1845, and we may see from the programme how proud the city was. How colourful the scene must have been inside, lit by the five great gas chandeliers! Manchester enjoyed the first performance of many plays, either because then as now plays put on in Manchester were pre-London rehearsals which gave time for further polishing, or because what Manchester applauds today, London will applaud to-morrow. Henry Irving, the great Shakespearian actor, first appeared at the Theatre Royal in 1860 during Charles Calvert's great period, when Shakespeare's plays were being produced with increased splendour and accurate costume and setting.

Charles Calvert also made the Prince's Theatre famous. It was situated where Peter House now stands in Oxford Street. In 1881 Irving appeared again as Shylock. At a banquet given in his honour, recalling his earlier struggle to make himself a success, he realised that then he was 'too raw, too unacceptable a fellow', but the Manchester audience saw his promise and gave him encouragement. The Prince's was for long the home of musical comedy such as that associated with George Edwardes' Gaiety Girls from London.

In the 1840s pantomime became firmly associated with Christmas, though it did not form the whole presentation until the 1870s. By this time in Manchester three separate productions could be seen in the city, and other towns such as Oldham and Bolton had their

# NEW  THEATRE ROYAL,

## PETER-STREET, MANCHESTER.

The Proprietor has great pleasure in informing the Public, that the following persons have been employed in the construction of the Theatre, under the immediate direction and superintendence of

### MESSRS. IRWIN & CHESTER.

## THE ENTIRE OF THE STRUCTURE BY MESSRS. PAULING & HENFREY,

CROSS-STREET, MANCHESTER.

**DECORATIONS & GILDING,** - - **GEORGE JACKSON,**

BRAZENNOSE STREET, MANCHESTER.

**ACT DROP,** - - - - **W. R. BEVERLEY.**

**UPHOLSTERY, &c.** - - - **W. D. FULLALOVE.**

KING STREET, MANCHESTER.

**GAS FITTINGS,** - - - **SUDLOW & BERRY,**

MARKET PLACE, MANCHESTER.

**GLASS CHANDELIERS,** - - **THOMAS AGNEW,**

EXCHANGE STREET, MANCHESTER.

**HEATING & VENTILATING,** - - **W. WALKER,**

LOWER KING STREET, MANCHESTER.

**PAPER HANGINGS,** - - - **CUFFLEY & HEIGHWAY,**

CROSS STREET, MANCHESTER.

**ARCHITECTS,** - - - - **IRWIN & CHESTER,**

84, FOUNTAIN STREET, MANCHESTER.

The Public is respectfully informed that the Theatre will be

# OPENED FOR THE SEASON,

## On MONDAY, SEPT. 29, 1845,

When will be performed the last new Comedy by DOUGLAS JERROLD, Esq., entitled

# TIME WORKS WONDERS.

To conclude with the new divertisement of a

# COURT BALL IN 1740,

## IN WHICH WILL BE REPRESENTED THE

# VARIOUS DANCES,

AS PERFORMED AT HER MAJESTY'S "BAL COSTUME."

Balls and Dress Circle, 4s.; Upper Circles, 2s. 6d.; Pit, 1s. 6d.; Gallery, 1s.; Upper Gallery, 6d.

**SECOND PRICE AT THE TERMINATION OF AN ACT ABOUT NINE O'CLOCK.**

Balls and Dress Circle, 2s.; Upper Circles, 1s. 6d.; Pit, 1s.; Gallery, 6d.

LOWES & CO., PRINTERS, 28, BOND-STREET, MANCHESTER.

*Announcement of the opening of the new Theatre Royal, 1845*

resident pantomimes. A group of outstanding producers (Julian Wylie is an example) now directed the development of pantomime, encouraging a return to the timeless stories based on fairy tales and nursery rhymes. At first dialogue had been barred but now local and topical comment added great liveliness. For instance in 1865, after the end of the American Civil War and the cotton famine which it caused in Lancashire, characters called Famine, Discord, Peace and Plenty appeared. Famine makes his exit, defeated, saying:

> And when I heard that cotton was so dear
> I stalked abroad and thought to inspire fear;
> But they, not daunted, sir, got up a fund,
> And fed the people, till I, fairly stunn'd,
> Was forced to retreat as if I'd been kicked
> And by that fund famine was fairly licked.

Like *Punch* with its satire, pantomime and music hall often presented a sharp social commentary on the times. Songs were also important, especially the rousing choruses. The tradition of female principal boys and male dames brought on to the pantomime stage great artists such as Vesta Tilley, Jean Adrienne, Dan Leno and George Robey. Dan Leno, so clever as a character actor, made each of his dames an individual performance. Pantomime is still vigorous, often using northern comedians, such as Ken Dodd and Morecambe and Wise (5).

## CHARLES DICKENS IN MANCHESTER

Charles Dickens visited Manchester on many occasions, and although he had hard things to say about industrial Lancashire's dirt, poverty and cruel factory masters in *Hard Times*, as an actor and reader of his own books he was very popular. His connections with Manchester are recalled by F. R. Dean in *The Dickensian* for March 1938. Dickens gives us the better side of the Manchester business man in the characters of the Cheeryble brothers in *Nicholas Nickleby*, based on two real brothers whom he met in Manchester. Dickens appeared in many plays – perhaps the most notable being *The Frozen Deep*, a drama written by Wilkie Collins, of which the author said: 'At Manchester the play was twice performed, the second evening in the presence of three thousand spectators. . . . The extraordinary intelligence and enthusiasm of the great audience stimulated us to do our best. Dickens surpassed himself. The trite phrase is the true phrase to describe that magnificence of acting – he electrified the audience.' This play was performed in the new Free Trade Hall built in 1856, of which the present building is a reconstruction. It was used for many different kinds of entertainment, including dancing.

*Playbill showing a part played by Dickens at the Free Trade Hall*

# FREE TRADE HALL.

UNDER THE MANAGEMENT OF MR. CHARLES DICKENS.

## ON MONDAY EVENING, AUG. 24th, 1857,

AT SEVEN O'CLOCK EXACTLY,

(By ten minutes before which time the whole audience is respectfully and particularly requested to be seated),

Will be presented an entirely New Romantic Drama, in Three Acts, by

### MR. WILKIE COLLINS,

CALLED

# THE FROZEN DEEP.

The Overture composed expressly for this Piece by Mr. FRANCESCO BERGER, who will conduct the Orchestra.

*The Dresses by* MESSRS. NATHAN, *of Titchbourne-street, Haymarket, and* MISS WILKINS, *of Carburton-street, Fitzroy Square. Perruquier,* MR. WILSON, *of the Strand.*

| | | | |
|---|---|---|---|
| CAPTAIN EBSWORTH | ... | (of the " Sea Mew") ... | MR. EDWARD PIGOTT. |
| CAPTAIN HELDING... | ... | (of the " Wanderer") ... | MR. ALFRED DICKENS. |
| LIEUTENANT CRAYFORD | ... | ... ... ... ... ... | MR. MARK LEMON. |
| FRANK ALDERSLEY ... | ... | ... ... ... ... ... | MR. WILKIE COLLINS. |
| RICHARD WARDOUR | ... | ... ... ... ... ... | MR. CHARLES DICKENS. |
| LIEUTENANT STEVENTON | ... | ... ... ... ... ... | MR. YOUNG CHARLES. |
| JOHN WANT... | ... | ... ... (Ship's Cook) ... | MR. AUGUSTUS EGG. |
| BATESON } DARKER } | ... | . .(two of the "Sea-Mew's" people)... | { MR. SHIRLEY BROOKS. { MR. CHARLES COLLINS. |

(OFFICERS AND CREWS OF THE " SEA-MEW" AND " WANDERER.")

| | | | |
|---|---|---|---|
| MRS. STEVENTON | ... | ... ... ... ... ... | MRS. GEORGE VINING. |
| ROSE EBSWORTH | ... | ... ... ... ... ... | MISS ELLEN SABINE. |
| LUCY CRAYFORD | ... | ... . ... ... ... ... | MISS ELLEN TERNAN. |
| CLARA BURNHAM | ... | ... ... ... ... ... | MISS MARIA TERNAN. |
| NURSE ESTHER | ... | ... ... ... ... ... | MRS. TERNAN. |
| MAID ... | ... | ... ... . ... ... ... | MISS MEWTE. |

The Scenery and Scenic Effects of the First Act, by MR. TELBIN.
The Scenery and Scenic Effects of the Second and Third Acts, by MR. STANFIELD, R.A., assisted by MR. CUTHBERT.

## MISS HORNIMAN'S REPERTORY COMPANY

In the 1890s Manchester welcomed the new revolutionary drama and established its own Independent Theatre Committee. From 1894 to 1898 the plays of Ibsen and Shaw were to be seen at the Gentlemen's Concert Hall in Peter Street. Plays like Shaw's *Candida* formed part of the repertoire of Manchester's greatest theatrical enterprise, Miss Horniman's Repertory Company which performed from 1908 to 1921 at the Gaiety Theatre (demolished in 1959), in Peter Street. Great actors such as Basil Dean, Lewis Casson and Sybil Thorndike took part with Miss Horniman in a plan to provide an enterprising and quickly changing programme, by which they hoped to attract an audience which would support their new approach to drama. This concentrated on brisk performances at popular prices instead of relying on a great star to provide the attraction. Miss Horniman also put on special shows for children. Three local authors, Stanley Houghton, Harold Brighouse and Allan Monkhouse, emerged whose plays were encouraged by this Manchester workshop. The virtues and vices of the industrial north were revealed in the plays of these three in humour and poignancy. A scene is shown (page 24) from *Hindle Wakes*, a famous Lancashire comedy by Stanley Houghton, put on in London and abroad as well as Manchester. When first produced by Lewis Casson in 1912 this play caused a stir in newspapers, pulpits and private discussion. The story tells of a Lancashire mill girl who goes away for a weekend with her employer's son. The Establishment decides the only proper course is marriage, but Fanny has other ideas. Some critics deplored 'the cool way in which possible maternity is kept out of sight', but after a London performance the *Daily Telegraph* generously found it 'a very remarkable performance of a very remarkable play, with admirable dramatic instinct, fine appreciation of character and a close study of Lancashire life'. Unfortunately Houghton only lived a further eighteen months.

Miss Horniman's experiment was the first repertory theatre in Great Britain and had a world influence – Lilian Baylis said it had a great effect on her and led her to start the Old Vic Company in London. A very large number of Miss Horniman's actors and actresses – Sybil Thorndike is an example – went on to still greater achievements later (6).

DRAMA TODAY

The war and financial difficulties brought the enterprise to a close in 1921. The Rusholme Theatre and the Manchester Playgoers' Club kept the repertory movement alive between the wars, supporting the movement for a civic theatre, and many amateur dramatic and operatic societies continue to flourish, including a special theatre for children based at Stretford. The Curtain Theatre at Rochdale, and the Little Theatres at Wigan and Bolton flourished in the absence of professional theatres. Many theatres were turned into cinemas in the twentieth century, including the Theatre Royal in 1920 and the Gaiety in 1921, and serious drama is now only intermittently seen in Manchester. There are now only two commercial theatres in Manchester, the Palace and the Opera House, the latter in financial difficulties. The Library Theatre, established in 1934 by the Libraries Committee and used at first by amateur companies and for lectures, has paid for itself and provided a venturesome repertoire for a series of talented companies since 1947. There is still a theatre in Salford, the home of Walter Greenwood and Shelagh Delaney, and the Oldham Repertory Company has made a name for itself. Yet for a period it seemed that a depression had settled on the live arts in Manchester and district.

In 1966 two events indicated something of a revival. A new theatre was built as part of the facilities of the Manchester University Drama Department, while also housing a resident repertory company and performing to the public. Dame Sybil Thorndike ('Who else could we possibly ask?' said Hugh Hunt, Professor in the Department) at the opening ceremony recalled the excitement of working at the Gaiety and hoped that in this new theatre also plays would 'pierce and stun and elevate' human emotions by that reaction which the live theatre can best stimulate. This theatre has all the latest mechanical improvements for adapting the stage, pit and auditorium for different kinds of performance.

Secondly, proposals are now in an advanced stage of discussion for a new Arts Centre in Manchester in the area between Oxford Street and Piccadilly always associated with entertainment. The plan includes a large opera house to seat 1,650, with resident opera and ballet companies, a theatre which Granada TV has offered to run as a training school for its producers, a film centre where experimental and classical films can be seen (supported by the British Film Institute), smaller halls and restaurants. The Minister for the Arts, Miss

Jennie Lee, has given (1967) enthusiastic support, and a government grant is likely if economic restrictions permit. Very many local cultural societies have joined forces in a new association to support the project. Sir Philip Dingle, formerly Town Clerk of Manchester, has expressed the North-west's strong claim to a larger share of the nation's subsidies to the fine arts from which London has so far benefited too much. The living audience will continue to be found for the live arts, especially if the skill of architects and designers can focus attention on a fine new set of buildings. Plans are also under consideration for an arts centre in Rochdale and form part of Graeme Shankland's imaginative scheme for the centre of Bolton, where the exciting new Octagon Theatre was opened in 1967. Where can you see real actors and actresses, singers or musicians at work? The thrill of participation in a great dramatic occasion, whether it be music, ballet, opera or plays, takes us out of ourselves. We all enjoy 'a reet good do' on a night out with our friends or family.

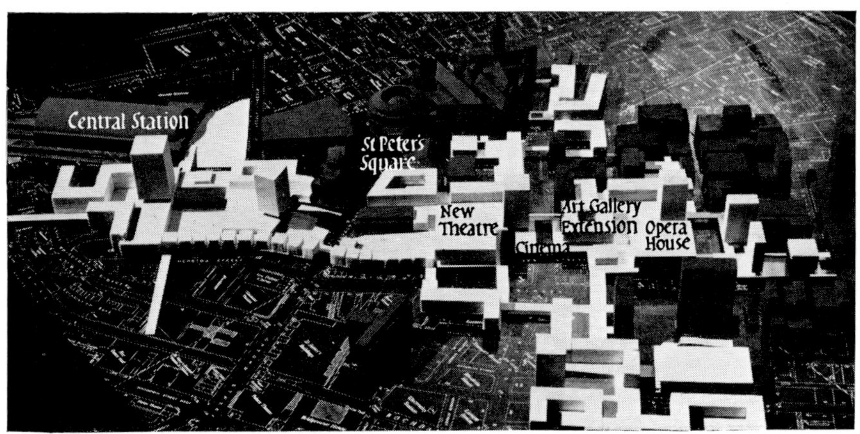


*Manchester's proposed Arts Centre*

# 3 Musical entertainments

Manchester concert audiences have often received tributes for their generous but also critical attitude. Sir John Barbirolli has paid many compliments to them and it is this loyalty and genuine love of music which has kept him in the North with the Hallé Orchestra despite many attractive offers from outside. An artist however has to prove himself in order to be accepted. Sir John gave an amusing illustration of this in a recent television programme. A soldier on leave came to him for an autograph at the interval, since he had to leave before the end of the concert. Asked how he liked the programme, he replied: 'Very good – so far.' In other words he was suspending judgment till he had heard more of the orchestra's work. But once the audience has accepted a performer they respond in the true warm-hearted northern way.

Our region has produced many performers of world stature. Isobel Baillie, the famous soprano, though born in Scotland, spent most of her life in Manchester and still keeps up her association with the city. Her talent was spotted when she was at school by a wise Manchester headmaster. Kathleen Ferrier in her tragically short but wonderful life as a singer always remembered her home town Blackburn and showed all that was best in Lancashire warm-hearted kindliness and modesty. At the peak of her career in the early 1950s, Neville Cardus, music critic of the *Guardian*, called her the most beautiful of all singers of her time – and this meant not her looks alone. Now John Ogdon who was brought up in Manchester and trained as a pianist at the Royal Manchester College of Music has received tumultuous acclaim in Moscow, home of his greatest rival

*John Ogdon at the piano, 1962*

Ashkenazy, and been presented with a wonderful piano for his outstanding achievement for British music. Truly the native talent and love of music are still flourishing, and the great training institutions, the Royal Manchester College of Music and Northern School of Music, will soon, it is hoped, unite in a magnificent new building including an auditorium adequate to their status as part of the new Education Precinct in Manchester.

This love of song and music included amateur performance as well as mere listening. It was often expressed in church and chapel where instrumentalists and choirs performed their own compositions as well as the sacred music of the masters. As one writer put it, 'Music was in the soul of the people, sweetening the toil of the day.' Wigan and Bolton have had a strong musical tradition in the nineteenth and twentieth centuries. The Rossendale players used to meet in each other's houses for rehearsals, and put all their best effort into the anniversary service at church and chapels, when the girls appeared in all their finery at the front of the platform with the male choir behind them. Many small Lancashire and Cheshire villages as well as towns had excellent choirs (for example, Shaw near Rochdale), but little has been recorded of their achievements.

## JESTERS AND MINSTRELS

In earlier days some of the great houses of Cheshire and Lancashire kept their own musicians and players including a jester. Manchester included among its officials up to four waits, or town minstrels. These are first referred to in 1563. They attended at weddings, dinners and played in the streets. At the festivities for the coronation of Charles II in 1661, when the fountain which usually provided the town's water ran with claret, the procession was headed by the waits playing on loud instruments. Minstrels from other places or wandering players were driven out of town or fined. In 1819 a petition to the magistrates in Manchester complained of the 'nuisance of profane and debauched ballad singing'. Wandering pipers were frowned upon as they tended to disturb church services and draw the rabble together. But the ballad singers provided entertainment for many who had little to amuse them.

One of the oldest Lancashire ballads, dating from the sixteenth century, preserved by Harland (7), tells the story of Gilbert Scott who sold his mare Barry at 'Warrikin' (Warrington) Fair, and had the greatest difficulty in getting his money. His wife Grace, a stronger character, went to the fair to waylay the purchaser.

'My gud mon', quo' hoo, 'Gilbert greets you right merry,
And begs that yo'll send him th' money for Barry.'

'Oh, money!' quo' he, 'that connot I spare:'
'Be lakin,' quo' hoo, 'then I'll ha' th' mare.'
Hoo poo'd an'hoo thrumper'd him sham' to be seen,
'Thou hangman,' quo' hoo, 'I'll poo' out thy e'en.'
So between 'em they made sich a wearisom' din,
That to mak' 'em at peace, Rondle Shay did come in.

'Cum, fye, naunty Grace; cum, fye an' ha' dun;
You'st ha' th' mare, or th' money, whether yo' won.'
So Grace geet th' money, an' whomwards hoo's gone;
But hoo keeps it hursel' an gies Gilbert Scott none.

(Poo'd = pulled; thrumper'd, a very expressive word = thumped; naunty = aunty, used familiarly. Rondle Shay was Sir Thomas Butler's bailiff for whom the purchaser of the mare worked.)

Some of the modern serious ballads are following an old tradition in talking about first love, the pleasures of food and drink, or loneliness.

SOUNDING BRASS

In the mid-nineteenth century a brass band fever swept the region. These bands were the working man's orchestra. Keen rivalry arose between the many towns in local competitions, leading eventually to the grand national contest which started in 1900 at the Crystal Palace. One of the earliest was at Stalybridge, where in 1815 a band played at the pace-egging festival just before Easter and later performed at foundation-stone ceremonies. It even became involved at Peterloo where it was to play for Orator Hunt; the bandsmen were warned in time not to become involved in any trouble that might start. A centenary history of the band was published in 1914.

Joseph N. Hampson in his book *The origin, history and achievements of the Besses o' th' Barn Band* shows how it was loved by its supporters.

Between seven and eight o'clock, on an evening when the band is away at the contest, any stranger passing through the village would wonder what was the cause of so many small groups of people standing here and there in the roadside. . . . They were talking about 'eawr band'. . . . When the result is known 'They've wun th' first agen', a smile of satisfaction and delight lights up the faces.

In 1888 for instance the band won all ten contests for which it entered.

The whole story of the development of the band from reed to brass, the start of the contests at Belle Vue in 1852 and the organising of railway excursions to them, the fierce rivalry between Lancashire and Yorkshire, the type of music played and instruments used, and the many great characters who took part, is given in a very lively way in J. F. Russell and J. H. Elliot's book *The brass band movement* (8). Though the movement was supported by the richer classes, because it kept the 'hands' out of mischief, conditions for acquiring an instrument or practising were not always easy – instruments often were patched with sticking plaster or smeared with soap to stop up the holes and rehearsals sometimes took place before the knocker-up went on his rounds. But enthusiasm was very great.

The major brass band contests of the late nineteenth century were tremendous popular attractions; thousands of working people assembled at each big meeting. No fewer than fifty excursion trains brought enthusiasts from all parts of the north to the Belle Vue September contest of 1888, which may be taken as typical. There were 8,000 people present when the contest began at one p.m. Thirty-five bands played the test-piece – a selection from *The Flying Dutchman*.

Among the audience, enthusiasm ran wild; the applause that greeted a band as it took up its position was exceeded only by the stamping and cheering that acknowledged its performance. Private comments were freely exchanged; each man was his own adjudicator; and dozens of band followers remained unbudgeable in their seats throughout the long hours of the contest, refreshing themselves from obscure packages bulging out of their pockets and less mysterious bottles tightly clipped between their ankles.

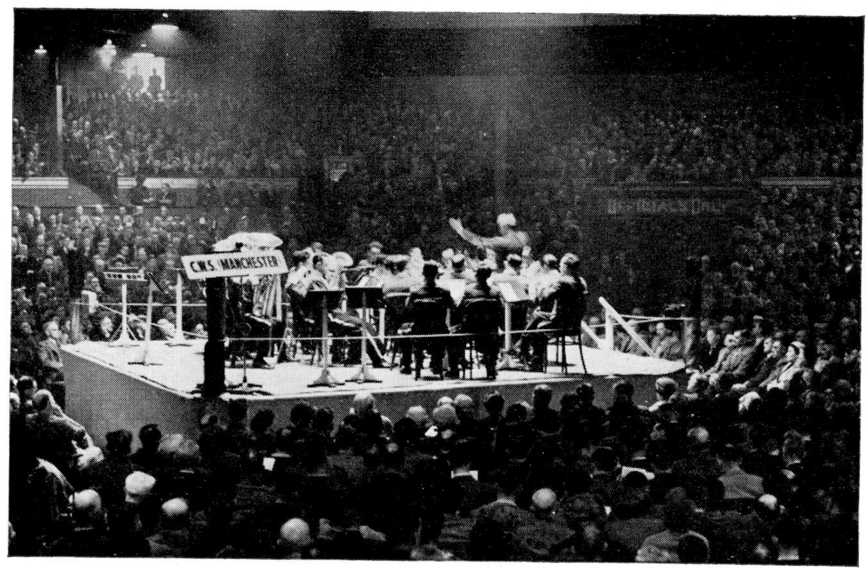

*A brass band contest at King's Hall, Belle Vue*

The appeal of sounding brass was also turned to their own use by such bodies as the temperance movement, and the Salvation Army.

MORRIS DANCING

Also associated with music were the morris dancers. The word *morris* may mean Moorish, deriving from the North Africans in Spain. This would perhaps explain the costume. In the North-west in the 1890s this consisted of decorated clogs, white stockings and black knee breeches tied with ribbons and bells at the knee, a bright sash round the waist, white shirts and white straw hats decorated with ribbons and rosettes. These were worn by the men; women did not take part. The dancers twirled flexible slings, or 'mollies' – rigid staffs tied with ribbons. Some of the dances tell a story, for example a mock fight. Their music was originally from pipe and tabor, later from a band consisting of concertinas, flutes and drums. In the North-west a special tradition of dancing grew up which was still being danced by over thirty teams in the early 1900s, being passed on by the leaders of the teams from the older forms connected with wakes celebrations and rushbearing. These old forms represent the heyday of the dance, which declined as the festivals disappeared.

The First World War and further changes in customs almost extinguished the morris dancers, but many remembered the costumes and steps. Here and there as at Knutsford in the 'Cranford' team new troupes were formed, and girls began to take part. Now morris dancing has become more popular again in the variety known as the Carnival Morris – more elaborate steps, performed mostly by girls in white gym shoes, with white blouses, coloured skirt, sash and shakers consisting of bundles of crepe papers bound tightly, spreading out the fuzz at each end. However, on the male side the Manchester morris men are thriving and at Bacup the Britannia Coconut Dancers perform special dances. They are called the Nutters because, having blackened their faces as a disguise, and wearing gay clogs, stockings, breeches, kilts, jerseys and plumed white caps, they beat wooden discs or nuts, which they wear on their hands, on other discs fastened to their knees and waists. Originally they danced their way between the boundaries of Bacup and Waterfoot and Whitworth on Easter Eve, preceded by a whipper-in who whipped away evil spirits. Now they have eight different dances which they perform for charities and on special occasions, accompanied by concertina or band music. There is a revival at present both of folk dancing such as this and of the old ballads and folksongs in which the region is rich. In fact the international magazine. *The Folk Musician and Singer*, was published in Manchester and the English Folk Dance and Song Society which organises festivals and helps to record and encourage the revival has a local association and holds many dances, training sessions and weekend courses. Lists are maintained of all places where dances are still performed or have been performed. From the same society a useful survey of the traditional Morris dance in the North-west (9)

*The 'Nutters' dancing at Bacup, 1967*

can be obtained, besides books and records which give the steps and tunes of the various types of dance. There are excellent pictures in its two booklets *Dances of England* and *Dancers of England*.

ORCHESTRAL AND CHORAL MUSIC

For those in Manchester interested chiefly in classical music, the Gentlemen's Concerts were founded in the eighteenth century. Subscribers later had their own concert hall in Peter Street, near where the Midland Hotel is now. The orchestra consisted of fifty players and there was a long waiting list of subscribers in the late 1830s. There was also a Gentlemen's Glee Club founded in 1830 and a Manchester Choral Society (from 1833) with permanent members aiming at encouraging local talent in choral and concerted music, e.g. church and chapel choirs. The musical evening in the richer man's private house was popular when people had to provide most of their own entertain-

*The Gentlemen's Concert Hall, Peter Street, Manchester, 1831*

ment. The young man or lady was not considered accomplished unless he had a repertoire of song or instrumental music. To aid them there were many high class schools of dancing and music, and private tutors. When invited to dinner, the guests at a musical evening brought their own music and instruments, but left them in a little case in the hall, since it was not done to show you were too eager to perform.

## THE HALLE ORCHESTRA

Manchester owed much to the liberal way in which foreigners were accepted into the community. Many German musicians brought the highest skills and tried to make Manchester a home from home. The greatest of these was Sir Charles Hallé, born in a small town in Germany where music flourished and where his father was a conductor. A Manchester calico printer, Hermann Leo, invited him to Manchester from London to which he had fled from the revolution in Paris in 1848. Hallé was appointed to the conductorship of the Gentlemen's Concerts in 1849 at a salary of £120 per year. Most of the popular musical attention at this time was directed to vocal music

36

*Sir Charles Hallé*

*Sir John Barbirolli*

and brass bands. Hallé had to create a new orchestra recruited partly from the old, partly from outside, and build by his fine performances a large enough popular following for music of all kinds, especially orchestral, which he thought the finest of all. He did not reject choral music, performing many operas and founding the St Cecilia Society, a new choral society on German lines. When the Art Treasures Exhibition was projected for 1857, as described in the next chapter, Hallé was invited to provide on the musical side an orchestra to rival the artistic side of the Exhibition.

From this was born the Hallé Orchestra (10). Hallé had long maintained: 'Even among audiences composed chiefly of artisans and miners, I had again and again been struck by the keen discernment of good and bad and by the unquestionable musical talent commonly revealed. In the cultivation of choral music I had nowhere met their equal.' He was responsible for the foundation of the Royal Manchester College of Music. He died in 1895; his successors, Hans Richter, Sir Hamilton Harty, Sir Thomas Beecham and Sir John Barbirolli, have maintained the world-wide reputation of the Hallé Orchestra. The

Free Trade Hall in Manchester, rebuilt after the Second World War, now provides a setting worthy of Manchester's musical occasions, though opera and ballet still lack a permanent home. Sir John also had the highest regard for his audience, particularly in the difficult years after the Second World War when the Free Trade Hall was still in ruins from German bombs and concerts were given in many strange places, most often at King's Hall, Belle Vue, hitherto better known as a boxing stadium. He has said:

In Manchester I have found an audience willing to walk hand in hand with me and explore great music. The wonderful new audience we have built up at Belle Vue is of my own class, the lower middle class. . . . The way they have turned out in snow and fog has mattered to me a great deal, as I am rather a human person.

*The Hallé Orchestra playing in the new Free Trade Hall, Manchester*

*The People's, a Manchester music hall*
*in Lower Mosley Street, 1899*

# 4 Other popular amusements

From the Free and Easies or smoking concerts and the questionable songs and music of the public houses grew the music hall. This was popular entertainment at its most vigorous. Clever character drawing and wit were commonly found, and there was a very close contact between audience and performer. There were many famous halls in this district, e.g., the Star at Bolton, the Folly, Tivoli, Comedy and the People's in Manchester in which the great stars appeared and new ones were nurtured. It was at the tiny singing room called the People's on the site where the Midland Hotel is now that Harry Randall, a great comedian from the Middlesex Music Hall in London, spotted a young lad singing a song called 'Milk for the Twins'. This was Dan Leno, the most famous performer of all who because of his Command Performances came to be known as the King's Jester. He typifies all that was best in music hall. Always a solo performer, he had the audience helpless with laughter as he struggled with his collar and shirt or tried to keep his trousers up, or became entangled with the harp on which he was trying to play a solo. He became the queen of pantomime dames, a comic performer of the part of a scraggy female, best loved perhaps for his famous sketches as a Beefeater in the Tower longing for refreshment, or as an ice-cream seller, or railway guard. No one who saw him could ever forget the tiny wistful figure with the dimpled chin.

Perhaps the most famous local figure in the variety which succeeded true music hall is Gracie Fields (11), the Rochdale lass who when a half-timer in a cotton mill picked up the tricks of her future trade on

*Gracie receives the freedom of Rochdale on the Town Hall balcony, 1954*

visits to local music halls. Through the medium of radio she later made many of her songs world famous, the sentiment always being relieved by a touch of burlesque – her voice could make the most marvellous funny noises. Typical of her many songs, and illustrating the power of music hall songs to foster the virtues of the ordinary man, is 'In my little bottom drawer'. Here is part of the chorus:

> One bridal gown, one eiderdown,
> I've been saving up since eighteen ninety-four,
> Got me ribbons and me bows,
> And me these and thems and those,
> All packed up in my little bottom drawer.
>
> One baby's cot, one flower pot,
> Where I've planted a rambling rosebush for the door,
> Got a motto for the wall,
> It says 'Heaven 'elp us all',
> All packed up in my little bottom drawer.

Music hall songs do not look much on paper – the sauce and humour were put into them by clever acting and facial expression.

Music hall reached its peak in the 1890s before cinema and radio were known, when notable artists such as Marie Lloyd, George Robey and Vesta Tilley appeared in the many music halls in our region. The present Palace Theatre in Manchester was built originally in 1891 as a Palace of Varieties. In Peter Street, Manchester, near the Free Trade Hall a former Methodist chapel was converted in 1865 to become Alexandra Music Hall. The original galleries were kept, but the pulpit was turned into a stage. This later changed its name to the Folly, then to the Tivoli in 1879. Jugglers, illusionists, conjurors, hypnotists as well as singers and comedians appeared. Unlike the early shows in pubs, these shows were fit for ladies to see.

The cinema and radio eventually killed the music halls. The Tivoli was converted into a cinema in 1921 but was burnt down in 1927. An old man watching its demolition was questioned by a reporter. He pointed to its gallery, remembering how in the old days of music hall things got pretty rough on Saturday night. On one occasion the show was not too good, and the audience refused to be entertained. One poor chap, a comedian, they wouldn't have at any price, and after two verses and a few gags he went off. Before he got off a particularly ripe tomato came down from that spot above there (the gallery) and caught him beautifully on the neck. The memory was an unhappy one because that neck was his own.

## CIRCUSES

Before the films and television made the wonders of the natural world and of man commonplace, the great showmen of the past tried to present them to the people, especially in the great centres of population. In the days before well organised zoos there were visits of lions and tigers and other strange animals. Travelling groups of freaks, Siamese twins and midgets, and strange foreign peoples like the Aztecs were on show. In 1859 Jim Myers' Great Equestrian Company communicated the excitement of the Wild West; later, nigger minstrels were imitated. Circuses remained popular in the nineteenth century. Famous ones, such as Pablo Fanque's (see the cover picture), visited many local towns. In 1842 in Mount Street, Manchester, a wooden building called Cooke's Circus was erected for equestrian shows and for plays in which animals were included. Though Cooke later went bankrupt, this site was used by the many travelling circuses which set up in Manchester. Hengler's Circus in Great Bridgewater Street was more successful, showing equestrian acts, equilibrists, acrobats, clowns, performing cats, dogs and other animals. The programme was interspersed with exciting melodramas such as Dick Turpin's ride to York, or the comedy put on in 1903,

*The Village Wedding*, in which ruffianly tramps pursued by police interrupt the proceedings. During a scene when the stage was flooded with 'real water' a river picnic was spoilt as we see in the illustration.

PLEASURE GARDENS

Several botanic and zoological gardens were laid out to meet the scientific curiosity of the growing population of the region. From showing plants and trees and landscape the gardens went on to capture holiday and Sunday crowds by musical programmes, refreshments and spectacles. The oldest, Tinker's Gardens, in Collyhurst, was most famous for firework and balloon displays round about 1800. We have already described in the first chapter one show at Pomona Gardens (on the site where now Pomona Docks stand). These gardens with their dance halls and agricultural halls were famous for galas, fêtes, dances (the quadrille band being especially good), political meetings and all kinds of entertainment. Here for instance the acrobat Blondin wheeled a man in a wheelbarrow across a high slack wire. Belle Vue Gardens, founded in 1836, owed their growth to the Jennings family. These pleasure gardens became very popular, attracting excursion trains from many parts of the country. Grown-ups and children enjoyed seeing the great beasts and smaller creatures in captivity. From 1852 there were by the lake at Belle Vue most elaborate firework displays showing great battles and sieges. We have seen that brass band concerts were held there; dancing, entertainments such as all-in wrestling and refreshments still continue to be available on a huge scale. A great new ballroom was opened in 1960, the 'New Elizabethan'.

# EXCHANGE ROOM,

**MANCHESTER.**

## NOW EXHIBITING

### A MAGNIFICENT

# OXY-HYDROGEN

#### ACHROMATIC

# MICROSCOPE,

On the same scale as

### EXHIBITED IN LONDON,

*OFFERING A GRAND DISPLAY OF THE WONDERS OF*

### *The Microscopic World.*

*Among many interesting objects shown by this instrument is*

# A DROP OF WATER

*Immensely Magnified, and occupying a surface of*

# 180 square Feet,

Containing innumerable living Creatures, Animalculæ, and Water Insects, among which the extraordinary

### *Living Skeleton Insect.*

THE WONDERS OF NATURE AND ENGINEERING:
MUSEUMS AND EXHIBITIONS

Institutions such as the Mechanics' Institutes, Literary and Philosophical Societies, Geological Societies, or Botanical and Horticultural Societies, encouraged a sense of wonder and an interest in the natural world. An ever growing number of people satisfied their curiosity by meetings and by establishing permanent museums. For instance the present Manchester Museum started in Peter Street when the Manchester Society for the Promotion of Natural History (founded 1821) collected birds, animals and insect specimens. From time to time the public was given a chance to see an unusual sort of magic lantern, a projection microscope, which the poster describes. It is perhaps surprising that scientific and engineering ingenuity was not more used in nineteenth-century entertainment, though now the travelling fairs and amusement parks such as that at Belle Vue show plenty of mechanical amusements.

An interesting anticipation of the big dipper was the centrifugal railway shown on page 46. Richard Roberts, engineer in the great Manchester firm of Sharp Roberts & Co., after succeeding with a model, set up this railway at the Mechanics' Institute as a working model, large enough to give thrills to his students in the 1840s, and pleasure to many spectators. You sat in the car, gained speed down the slope and whizzed round twice on the eighty-foot wheel in the middle before slowing down again in the upgrade – thus showing the power of centrifugal force which prevented you from falling out of the car.

Exhibitions to show the ordinary people as well as the trade the fine products of industry and science have been organised for over a hundred years. The Royal Jubilee Exhibition, celebrating fifty years of Queen Victoria's reign, in 1887 demonstrated the ability of our great-grandfathers to plan such big shows in the exuberant manner of the

time. Robert Neill and Sons erected huge pavilions near the Botanic Gardens in Old Trafford, gardens were laid out, fountains played and an elaborate musical programme for the organ and for brass bands was planned. The largest area ever used for machinery up to that date impressed the four and three-quarter million visitors who came between May and November. Many societies met at the Exhibition. A profit of £43,000 was made, which contributed to the cost of the new technical and art colleges in Manchester, and the Whitworth Art Gallery.

ART GALLERIES

Many movements, started privately in the late eighteenth and early nineteenth centuries to amuse and instruct, later became part of the recreational facilities of the region paid for through the rates.

Of these the Royal Manchester Institution is a good example. It started in 1823 and aimed 'to show this opulent and populous district the best models of painting and sculpture'. Its building, now the City Art Gallery, was designed by Barry, the famous architect, responsible also for the Houses of Parliament. Lectures on scientific matters as well as literature and art were started; autumn became the time for exhibitions of painting and sculpture. Evening opening became possible in 1838, when gas lighting was introduced. Because of financial difficulties and lack of purchasing power for new exhibits the Institution was taken over by Manchester Corporation on condition that at least £2,000 per annum be spent on works of art. Since then a fine collection of work by British artists of the last 250 years has been built up. Do you know what is in your nearest Art Gallery and Museum and how they came to be built?

## THE ART TREASURES EXHIBITION 1857

Perhaps the finest hour of the old RMI was the Art Treasures Exhibition of 1857. The idea was supported by the Prince Consort who wanted to do for art what the Great Exhibition of 1851 in London had done for science and industry. A wonderful collection of pictures was assembled from many private and public collections all over the world; huge pavilions of iron and glass were designed by Edward Salomans; even a special station with standing room for empty trains was erected on the site at Old Trafford. Our Victorian ancestors were great organisers.

The exhibition was a great success, the Queen herself visiting it on 30 June. The crinolines worn by the ladies were so wide that the turnstiles were choked and put out of action and wider gates had to be made. A special exhibition was held in 1957 at the City Art Gallery to commemorate the centenary of this great event.

## FURTHER INDOOR AMUSEMENTS

The various Assembly Rooms in Manchester were available for such functions as balls and dances. The earliest, built in 1792, had a ballroom eighty-seven by thirty-four feet, tea room, card room and billiard room. A notice said: 'The tickets for dancing to be distributed a quarter before eight. Dancing to begin at eight. Ladies to take their places according to the numbers of their tickets and to keep them during the evening. Gentlemen to change partners every two dances.'

The picture shows one of the finest interiors of any building in Manchester, the Assembly Rooms in Cheetham, now demolished. This building, opened in 1859, had one of the first sprung dance floors in the country and a perfumed air ventilation system.

Modern indoor amusements are somewhat different. Bridge, chess, billiards and the later game snooker, ballroom dancing, ice skating (for which Manchester has long been well provided, most recently with the modernised ice rink at Cheetham and a new rink in Altrincham), and roller skating are established. The newer games of tenpin bowling and bingo show trends which are not of local origin and Manchester has become a centre for night clubs and gambling. A metropolis attracts both the worst and the best in entertainment.

*Ball at the Assembly Rooms, Manchester, on the opening night*

# 5 Cinema: radio: television

15, OXFORD STREET

THE MOST WONDERFUL
Invention of the 19th Century is

EDISON'S
KINETOSCOPES.

Electricity & Photography
Combined.

Marvellously re-produces Life-like Actions.
1,200 DISTINCT MOTIONS OF LIFE
Are seen in 24 Seconds of Time
1d. Each.

Cinema developed from the early dioramas and panoramas which depended on optical illusions and photographic inventions to give the effect of depth and movement. In our area, the various stages in this process can be traced in the shows put on for audiences (who by 1900 had much more leisure). The Edison Kinetoscope, which gave the illusion of movement through a series of pictures viewed through a slot, was shown in 1894 as we see from the poster. After the inventions of Lumière in 1895 the true cinematograph picture became possible. The *Manchester Guardian*, reviewing the first show at the Free Trade Hall on 20 May 1896, in a tiny paragraph tucked under the football news, mentioned scenes at a Lyons factory with all the bustle and activity that mark departure at meal times. Bicyclists mount their machines and ride off through the laughing crowd. It comments on the clear representation of minute detail and the lack of colour but does not appreciate this was the eve of a revolution in entertainment. In 1901 the Thomas–Edison Animated Photo Co. brought 'for the first time in the history of the world Actual Battle Scenes in progress to your very doors'. These were pictures of the China and Boer Wars together with local items such as the Whit Monday procession and the Catholic procession and the Lord Mayor opening the new electric car system (trams). Biograph Animated Photographs offered on film 'An ideal Xmas Programme of Mirth, Music and Mystery, Picture, Song and Story' in that same year.

D

The first picture houses were improvised in existing halls but so popular was this new entertainment that by 1911 in Manchester fourteen picture 'palaces' had been built – the name suggesting the glamour of the glittering screen and lush fittings. Some early programmes survive; for instance, one at the Oxford Picture House lists short films on making steel, current events, a Keystone comedy and the Edison kinetophone – the first attempt at talking pictures, invented in 1891, which combined Edison's phonograph (or record player) with forty feet of film wound on bobbins, the two working together. The rest of the programme was accompanied by an orchestra playing selections appropriate to the silent pictures. At first cinema-going was regarded as 'not quite the thing' and serious reviews in national papers were rare till the 1920s.

The cinema reached its peak as an entertainment in the period between the wars. Many theatres such as the Gaiety in Manchester, the Theatre Royal in Bolton, and the Royal Court in Wigan could no longer find audiences and were converted into cinemas. The attraction of cinema organs in the huge new cinemas of the 1930s was added to films which by now included sound and colour. The first sound film in Manchester was *Uncle Tom's Cabin* shown in 1928 at the New Oxford Cinema. By 1934 in Manchester there were 109 cinemas large and small, and every other town was well supplied. The Rex Cinema, Salford, shown on page 51, opened in 1938, is a good example of the style of building. Prices were low and children's matinées were common; teachers complained that children visited the cinema three or four evenings a week and did not do their homework properly. The opening of a new cinema was an important local event. A typical lush cinema seating 884 in the circle and 1,676 in the stalls was the Ritz at Wigan, opened by ABC in 1938 and still in use. The first film was Frank Capra's supreme achievement, *Lost Horizon*, with Ronald Colman, continuous from 2 p.m. to 10.45 p.m. weekdays with prices from front stalls (too near the screen) at 6d. to 1s. 10d. at the front of the circle.

A very interesting way to learn more of the history of the cinema and its personalities is to read *Thank you for having me* (12), the autobiography of C. A. Lejeune, the local-born film critic of *The Guardian* and *The Observer*. She did more than anyone to bring to the art of the film the appreciation it deserved.

By 1965 only forty cinemas remained in the City of Manchester. Most cinemas which survived the reduction in filmgoing were near town centres. Sunday opening and the various types of wide screen have not prevented the conversion of many cinemas into bowling alleys, warehouses, bingo clubs or TV studios. It would be interesting

*A Salford 'Picture Palace'*

for you to obtain a list from a directory of the 1930s of the names and addresses of all cinemas in your district, and to find what has happened to them now. Old cinema programmes and bills, opening brochures and photographs are extremely rare. Your local library would welcome any information you or your parents can give them.

Amateur societies have continued to show the great films of all ages. A special interest attaches to films with local settings, such as *A Taste of Honey*, *Hell is a City* and *A Kind of Loving*, and to films with local stars such as Albert Finney or Dora Bryan. There are signs that a balance is being achieved between the home entertainment of radio and TV on the one hand, and the socially more exciting and shared pleasures of the screen. Much of the art and experience of the film has of course been used in the new medium of television.

RADIO

Alongside the cinema a new form of sound entertainment developed, in which Manchester played an important part. This was radio. The experiments by the Marconi Company in 1920 were followed by the formation of amateur as well as official groups, including one at Manchester. Members played with unreliable crystal sets using 'cat's whiskers' – small crystals acting as simple rectifiers on which contact was made by a stiff wire like a cat's whisker. I well remember my father, one of the pioneers, who was called on to repair all our neighbours' wireless sets, sitting in our attic surrounded by base-boards of ebonite on which home-made tuning coils and other apparatus were linked by festoons of wire. Our aerial stretched to the house next door. I was allowed to manipulate the cat's whisker and listen through headphones to 2ZY, Manchester's call sign. Then it was common to call your best girl friend 'the real cat's whiskers'.

At the same time that R. D. Bangay and the enthusiastic P. P. Eckersley of the Marconi Company were broadcasting a weekly half

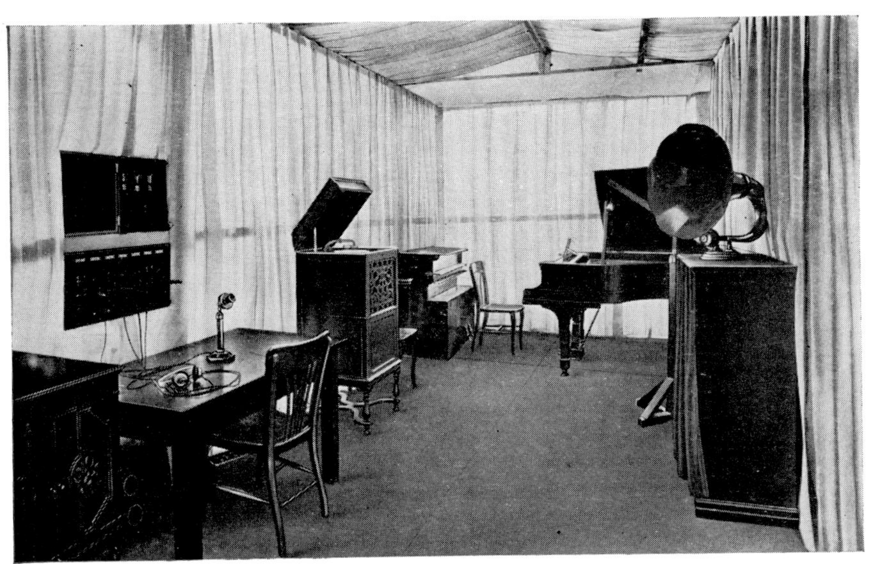



*Above: Manchester's first radio transmitting station, call sign 2ZY, 1922*
*Right : Cat's whiskers for sale*

hour programme for amateurs from Writtle near Chelmsford in Essex in 1922, the Metropolitan-Vickers Electrical Company in Trafford Park had set up a radio station in their research department. A.P.M. (later Sir Arthur) Fleming, who was head of this department, had become very enthusiastic about radio after a visit to the more highly developed broadcasting system in America. A conference room was turned into a studio with the aid of canvas partitions, joined by a multitude of wires to a transmitter under a staircase, and broadcasts went out through a cage-shaped aerial slung between a water tower and the top of the main building. Improvements were rapidly made to station 2ZY which rivalled 2LO at Writtle, and the company developed not only transmitters but also receivers. In fact by autumn 1922 their Cosmos crystal-type radiophone could be bought for £4 10s. Sets with valves were much more expensive, a two-valve set costing £26 10s. Much thought also was given to the content of the programmes – educational and children's programmes were regarded as important, and a weekly printed programme was recommended, the forerunner of *Radio Times*.

When the British Broadcasting Company was formed in October 1922, the Manchester station, with the others, was taken over, and the first official broadcast from the North took place on 15 November, the day after London began broadcasting. Conditions in the early days were rather primitive – a short singer had to stand on a pile of books to reach the microphone, which was not adjustable, and to get a whole band in the studio some bandsmen had to sit on the piano. The station was moved in 1924 to larger premises in Orme buildings, off Deansgate, but these in turn proved inadequate and in 1929 premises in Piccadilly were taken over which became Broadcasting House. Wireless was becoming ever more popular, more stations were opened, and more sets were bought or made at home. Advisory committees were set up to help the regional stations choose their programmes.

Peter Eckersley, Chief Engineer of the BBC till 1929, had the idea of regional broadcasting in which each region should present an alternative programme. The regions were to take from London part of their programmes, but add material which they could produce better themselves, including items of special local interest. Part of the regional plan was accomplished in 1931 when Moorside Edge, near Huddersfield, was opened as a new transmitting station, high up on the moors so that it could transmit to all the country south of the Scottish border and north of a line drawn from the Dee to the Wash, the largest of the regions. It broadcast on the longest medium wave allotted to the BBC by a plan agreed at a European Conference in 1929. Activities of other relay stations in the area were co-ordinated and a full regional coverage was built up. Such important local events as the opening of the Mersey Tunnel in 1934 and programmes from the coastal resorts helped to promote a regional unity, though to this day there is some difficulty in reconciling the interests of the rival urban populations of Manchester, Liverpool, Leeds, Sheffield and New-castle with the agricultural areas of Cumberland or Lincolnshire. The North Region under E. A. F. Harding as Programme Director rivalled London in the enterprise and interest of its programmes of talks, plays, features and music, put together with the aid of journalists trained on *The Guardian*, and notable broadcasters such as Wilfred Pickles.

The Northern Orchestra, formed in 1934 by the BBC, and still the BBC's second symphony orchestra, worked closely with the Hallé in providing musical entertainment, full advantage also being taken of the North's love of sounding brass and choral music. Amongst regional programmes of note 'The North Countryman' series explored the by-ways of local life and customs in the nine northern counties. One of its producers has described it as 'a programme about ordinary people for ordinary people. By and large its listeners are on the wrong side of forty, live in not too large towns, would prefer to live in the country and have a lively curiosity as to how other people like them find life.' Programmes were often in dialect which radio has fortunately helped to preserve. Three collections taken from this series have been published by the Dalesman Publishing Company, a northern enterprise. Northern stars such as Gracie Fields, Norman Evans and George Formby have made important contributions to radio entertainment.

Sound broadcasting has continued to be an important medium since the war despite the visual advantage of TV, helped by the development of cheap portable transistor radios, and the extension of the Very High Frequency network of transmitters over the whole country. These broadcasts cut out the interference which is frequent on medium-wave stations. Great efforts have been made to ensure good reception of all three radio programmes in our area. Lord Simon of Wythenshawe, Chairman of the BBC Board of Governors from 1947 to 1951, brought an independent business mind to its affairs as well as strong views on the educational possibilities of broadcasting. He was strongly opposed to commercial broadcasting on radio or TV. The region is proud of the contributions it has made to nation wide programmes, the patronage it has given to local talent, and the contribution to local news it makes in the nightly 'News of the North' programme (13).

TELEVISION

The most important post-war development in entertainment has been the growth of television studios and programmes from our region. As with broadcasting so in this new medium the North has developed its own sturdy independence. Manchester has become the home of the Northern Region Television Service of the BBC as well as the Headquarters of an independent television company, Granada, which serves the northern counties with weekday programmes. It is also the HQ for the North and Midlands of ABC Television which puts out week-end programmes in those regions.

The story of the start and success of Granada Television is almost like a fairy tale, with revenue from advertising taking the place of the traditional fairy godmother of the stories. The company began as an offshoot of a parent company already noted for its independence of mind in the way it ran its theatres and cinemas in the South of England. After the report of the Beveridge Committee, followed by long parliamentary debates concerned with whether the BBC should have a monopoly of TV and whether commercial advertising on TV was in the public interest, independent television was born in 1955. Granada was granted a contract for the northern week-day service and within a year the first building specifically designed as a studio was erected in Quay Street, Manchester. Staff and buildings grew together, a warehouse was taken over, training was arranged in London and the first programme went on the air on 3 May 1956. Within eight months a million homes were being reached which had receivers able to obtain both BBC and ITV and after a year the Granada audience had surpassed that of London in size.

The approach of Granada to its task was soon shown to be direct and down to earth. It had no great respect for precedent and was willing to take risks and experiment. It cultivated a deliberate northern outlook. Mr Sidney Bernstein, its chairman, has said: 'We prefer the North because of its home-grown culture, and because it offers the chance to start a new creative industry away from the metropolitan atmosphere of London.' He has cleverly fostered the image of 'Granadaland'. Programmes such as 'Under Fire', 'What the Papers Say' and 'Youth is Asking' showed how new ideas could be successful both with the more serious and the ordinary non-specialist viewers. Popular entertainment in the form of plays achieved a high level and

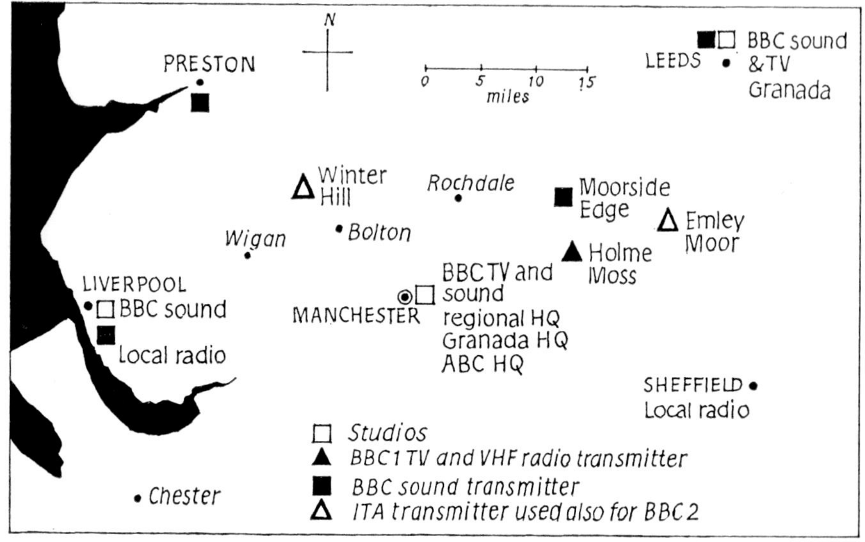


*The network of broadcasting transmitters and studios in the Manchester area, 1967*

local dramatists both old and new were used, not only writers of plays of the Horniman period but new authors such as Shelagh Delaney. The rich humour of Lancashire folk was presented larger than life in the series entitled 'Coronation Street', a place set in Salford which became more real than reality to viewers and for a long period was the most popular TV programme in the national ratings.

Granada exploited with its 'travelling eyes,' or mobile studios, local events such as the return of Manchester City with the Cup in 1956, and the Rochdale by-election of 1958 in which Ludovic Kennedy, himself a TV star, and Liberal candidate, split the Labour and Tory votes, pushing Tories to the bottom of the poll. Granada has stimulated other TV producers to be more interested in current affairs and elections, and has achieved some successes in feature and documentary programmes, for instance a series 'While the City Sleeps'. It has shown the exuberance of something new and succeeded in interesting viewers in wider realities and more imaginative films, art, and drama than critics had thought possible. It has not perhaps sufficiently fostered all the possibilities of programmes of local interest (14).

ABC Television, like Granada, started in 1956, having established studios at the former Capitol Cinema in Didsbury. Here was established its HQ for the North and Midlands and a base for its Outside Broadcast fleet. In 1962 fine new offices were opened in Manchester, partly on the site of the old Gaiety Theatre. A plaque in the new building commemorates Miss Horniman's Company. ABC programmes have been especially strong in drama, for instance the Armchair Theatre series. A link with the Extra-Mural Department of the University makes possible interesting developments in the instructive programmes so well suited to the medium of television – on, for example, cookery, do-it-yourself, art appreciation, or farming.

Both these commercial companies have supported the live arts locally. Granada has endowed the Professorships of Drama at Manchester and of Communication at Keele Universities, and encouraged local theatres, art galleries and musical festivals by grants. It encourages research into the arts of drama and television. ABC has supported local theatres, for instance the Library Theatre.

The BBC started its regional television service in 1951 from a transmitter at Holme Moss which is still its main transmitter. Its first permanent studios were in a converted church in Rusholme, opened in 1954. Later the Hulme Playhouse, formerly a repertory theatre, was taken over and is still used for shows with a live audience. In 1959 new studios more centrally placed in Piccadilly made topical and news programmes easier to produce. The main control room and switching centre for radio and TV remains there, but there are offices in Peter House, Oxford Street. In October 1965 BBC2 programmes began to be transmitted from the station at Winter Hill now shared with the ITA.

Without the stimulus of independence from London or a large

revenue from advertising, BBC northern TV developed some lively new programmes. Particularly popular was the gay weekly magazine on local topics 'Points North', now merged into the daily 'Look North' news programme which rivals 'Scene' on Granada TV. The region has perhaps been strongest in light entertainment on TV as on sound. It runs the Northern Dance Orchestra, helped to establish Ken Dodd, and began the Harry Worth show and 'Top of the Pops', both of which were taken over by London. The need for a large headquarters more at the heart of things is recognised by the Manchester City Council who have allocated a site in the Education Precinct for a proposed £4½ million building. There is a danger, however, that the BBC because it is more subject to public control will not be allowed to build and thus be unable to make its full contribution to northern entertainment.

Let us think, in conclusion, of the changing pattern of popular entertainment. We have seen that many of its elements remain the same over the ages – the attraction of the latest news and personalities, foreign scenes and wild beasts, the humour of the voice and face and acting of a comic, the tragedy of the human situation which, as Dame Sybil Thorndike has said, pierces us through great acting, the appeal of rhythm and music in song or dance or instrument. Each new medium has built upon what the old ways provided – the radio using the humour and variety of music hall, television using many of the arts of theatre and cinema. But each also brings something entirely new. Even the buildings made for entertainment are now put to new uses. The Hippodrome at Rochdale has been theatre, music hall and cinema and is now a bingo hall. Some buildings, like the Capitol Cinema in Didsbury, are used by the latest medium, television, where still a live audience is needed to which the performers can respond. But communal entertainments in special buildings are perhaps less important and less successful, and the centre of entertainment has become the lounge with its armchair and TV set. Do you think we have lost some vivid pleasures which our parents and grandparents enjoyed – the smell of the circus ring, the brilliance of a great gas chandelier, the jostling and full blooded response which they in the audience gave to the great actor or comedian? The number of hours of entertainment available on the different channels is enormous, but is the quality likely to be diluted, as each show must appear new? Have the producers fully used the wit and skill of our own local people in the way that local pantomime or the local fête or the local Morris team have done? Those of you who want to find out more will perhaps be helped by the list of further sources of information which follows.

*A 'Pinky and Perky' programme in production in the B B C Manchester studios*

Apart from local collections of books, pictures, newspaper cuttings and files of old newspapers in libraries, museums and art galleries frequently have interesting items (playbills, model theatres). The *Manchester Programme*, which advertised and commented rather rosily upon all forms of entertainment, is available in the Manchester Central Library for the years 1897 to 1934; *Events in Manchester* follows on after that date.


1 PRIESTNALL, J. and MITCHELL, W. E.   *The Play of St George, the Knights and the Dragon*   Privately printed, 1930.   (The text of the Mummer's Play as performed at Rochdale Grammar School for Boys.)

2 SOCIETY FOR THEATRE RESEARCH, MANCHESTER GROUP   *Exhibition: 200 years of theatres in Manchester* 1952.   (Includes notes on the more important theatres and lists chief theatres and music halls with their dates.)

3 LEACH, E.   'Playbills and programmes'   In *Manchester Review* Spring-Summer 1966   (An amusing account of the collection in the Manchester Arts Library and how the bill developed into a full programme.)

4 HODGKINSON, J. L. and POGSON, R.   *The early Manchester theatre*   Blond, 1960.   (Up to 1807.)

5 POGSON, R.   'The pantomime tradition'   *Manchester Review*   Winter 1955.

6 POGSON, R.   *Miss Horniman and the Gaiety Theatre, Manchester*   Rockliff, 1952.

7 HARLAND, J.   *Ballads and songs of Lancashire*   Enlarged by T. T. Wilkinson   John Heywood, 3rd ed. 1882.

8 RUSSELL, J. F. and ELLIOT, J. H.   *The brass band movement*   Dent, 1936.

9 HOWISON, D. and BENTLEY, B.   'The North West Morris'   Reprinted from the *Journal of the English Folk Dance and Song Society.*   December 1960.

10 KENNEDY, M.   *The Hallé Tradition*   Manchester University Press, 1960.

11 FIELDS, GRACIE   *Sing as we go*   Muller, 1960.

12 LEJEUNE, C. A.   *Thank you for having me*   Hutchinson, 1964.

13 BRIGGS, ASA   *A history of broadcasting*   (2 vols)   Oxford University Press, 1961 and 1965.   (Includes information about the North Region.)

14 GRANADA TELEVISION   *Year Ten*   1966.   (Gives an account of the chief programmes and lists all the staff.)   Several useful pamphlets are also available e.g. *What is a TV Centre?* 1966, and *Granada goes to Rochdale,* 1961.

References to illustrations
are shown in **bold type**

Blackburn
Darwen
Chorley
LANCASHIRE
Horwich
Bolton
A 6
Wigan
Farnwo
Tyldesley
M 62
E
Ashton-in-Makerfield
Leigh
Sa
St Helens
Newton-le-Willows
St
Liverpool
Warrington
Lymm
A
Widnes
Manchester ship canal
O Runcorn
M 6
River Mersey
Knu
Northwich
H
Chester
Middlewich